D1706798

MYSTERIES OF LIFE ON EARTH AND BEYOND

MYSTERIES OF THE UNIVERSE SERIES

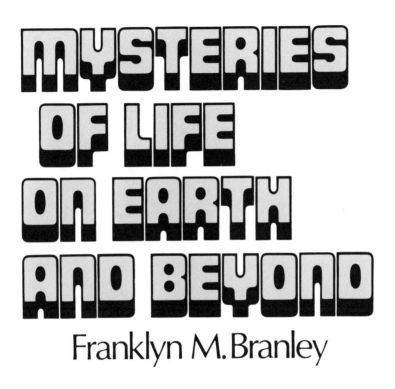

MYSTERIES OF LIFE ON EARTH AND BEYOND

Franklyn M. Branley

Diagrams by Sally J. Bensusen

LODESTAR BOOKS   E. P. DUTTON   NEW YORK

Text copyright © 1987 by Franklyn M. Branley
Illustrations copyright © 1987 by E. P. Dutton

Library of Congress Cataloging in Publication Data

Branley, Franklyn Mansfield, date.
  Mysteries of life on earth and beyond.

  (Mysteries of the universe series)
  "Lodestar books."
  Bibliography: p.
  Includes index.
  Summary: Explains present and future methods and technology used for the exploration of space and the search for life on other planets.
    1. Life on other planets—Juvenile literature.
  [1. Life on other planets. 2. Outer space—Exploration]
  I. Bensusen, Sally J., ill. II. Title. III. Series:
  Branley, Franklyn Mansfield, date. Mysteries of the universe series.
  QB54.B696 1987 574.999 86-19929
  ISBN 0-525-67195-1

Published in the United States by E. P. Dutton,
2 Park Avenue, New York, N.Y. 10016,
a division of NAL Penguin Inc.

Published simultaneously in Canada by
The New American Library of Canada Limited

Editor: Virginia Buckley   Designer: Riki Levinson

Printed in the U.S.A.   W   First Edition
10 9 8 7 6 5 4 3 2 1

CONTENTS

MYSTERIES OF LIFE ON EARTH AND BEYOND

"There's no use trying," [Alice] said: "one *can't* believe impossible things."

"I daresay you haven't had much practice," said the Queen. "When I was your age, I always did it for half-an-hour a day. Why, sometimes I've believed as many as six impossible things before breakfast."

Lewis Carroll,
Alice's Adventures in Wonderland

1 EARTH AMONG THE PLANETS

One day we'll solve the mysteries of life here on Earth as well as in the universe. We'll discover that there are people living on planets far beyond our solar system. The planets will be going around distant stars. They may be stars we can see easily in our night sky, or they may be stars too far away for us to detect. The people will be intelligent and able to send out radio waves. When we pick up those waves, we will know for certain that we are not alone in the universe.

That's what a good many scientists believe. Our galaxy is one of billions of galaxies in the universe, and each galaxy is made of billions of stars. So the total number of stars in the universe adds up to a staggering amount. A small percentage of those stars, but still amounting to millions, must have planets going around them. Among those millions of planets, these scientists say, there are many that support life—creatures that are just as intelligent as we are, or maybe more intelligent than we can imagine.

Not everyone agrees with this belief. We are certain about the number of stars in the universe, but we cannot prove that planets are going around any of them. Although there is no definite proof

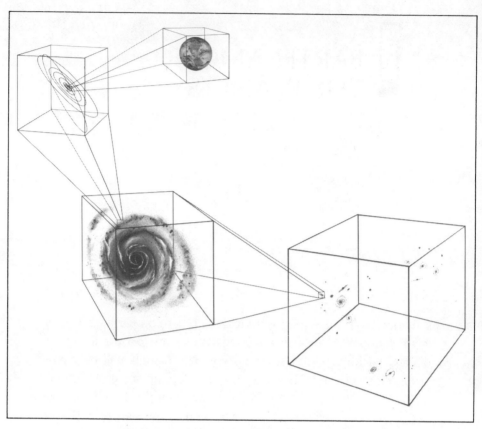

Our planet is one of nine in the solar system. The solar system is a speck located 30 000 light-years from the center of the Milky Way galaxy. The Milky Way belongs to a group of about twenty other galaxies, and this group is a tiny part of a universe which may extend for 15 billion light-years.

that such planets exist, observations of side-to-side movements of stars lead many to believe that planets are the cause. Many people question that there are intelligent beings somewhere beyond Earth, for in spite of many efforts to detect their presence, there is not the slightest evidence that life exists anywhere except on our own planet.

But in a report of programs for the 1980s, the National Academy of Science, an organization of the top scientists of our country, said:

> Intelligent organisms are as much a part of the universe as are stars and galaxies. Investigating whether some of the electromagnetic radiation now arriving at Earth was generated by intelligent beings in space may thus be considered a legitimate part of astronomy.

The most exciting event in the history of mankind would be the discovery of life on other worlds. If ever such a discovery is made, it will not come about by accident. Space must be explored energetically for the presence of life. In this book, we'll explain some of the ways we are doing this, the equipment being used, and the methods that may be tried in the future. Also, we'll take a look at space itself and see what it is made of, to explain why so many scientists believe there are creatures living on planets going around far-off stars. We'll begin with a survey of Earth.

How does Earth compare with the other planets?

Its size places Earth exactly in the middle—four of the planets are larger than we are, and four of them are smaller. In addition, the planets differ from one another in many ways.

Mercury and Pluto are the smallest—much smaller than we are. Jupiter, Saturn, Uranus, and Neptune are the major planets, and each is covered by dense gases. Also, each of these large planets may have rings. We know that Jupiter, Saturn, and Uranus do. Venus is extremely hot all the time, some 460° Celsius (C) both day and night. Mars has a diameter about half that of Earth. Presently it lacks abundant water. However, photographs reveal crustal waterways, which imply the planet probably had considerable water during some part of its history. As far as we know, none of these planets now, or ever, has contained living organisms.

Of all the planets, Earth seems to be the only one that supports

Mercury
(4880 km)

Venus
(12 100 km)

Earth
(12 756 km)

Mars
(6794 km)

Jupiter
(143 200 km)

Sun
(1 392 000 km)

Saturn
(120 000 km)

Uranus
(51 800 km)

Neptune
(49 500 km)

Pluto
(~3000 km)

At one time, people believed that bat-winged creatures, bear-like animals, and trees and other plants lived on the Moon.
COURTESY DEPARTMENT OF LIBRARY SERVICES, AMERICAN MUSEUM OF NATURAL HISTORY

life. This is a conclusion that was not made easily, for many people have long believed that there were living things elsewhere in our solar system, even though they could not prove it.

Has life ever existed on the Moon?

For hundreds of years, many people believed there were Moon people. In fact, in 1835, a newspaper printed a story describing the Moon people as having wings like those of a bat. The paper said that John Herschel, an English astronomer, had discovered them with his large telescope newly erected in South Africa.

He could see the Moon people eating melons by the edge of

◄ *In the solar system, Earth is middle-sized. Four of the nine planets are larger and four are smaller than Earth. The Sun is much larger than all the planets combined.*

a lake. Around them were birds and animals, some like small buffaloes and others that were bearlike. The story ran for six days in installments. Each day, people stood in line waiting for the paper to be printed. They wanted to get a copy so they could read about the latest discoveries. Although the story was not true, people believed it. The whole story was a hoax; it was a scheme used by the editor to increase sales of the newspaper.

By the 1960s, people no longer believed in lunar bat-men, but many still thought there were other forms of life on the Moon, life forms too small to see with telescopes. People were confident that if we ever explored the Moon firsthand, we would find microscopic forms of life or fossils of earlier life.

On July 20, 1969, Neil Armstrong became the first person to walk on the Moon. In the next several years, many more astronauts were to follow. Each mission returned samples of lunar rocks to Earth. The rocks were studied carefully by hundreds of scientists, to learn about the history of the Moon and, especially, to look for signs that some kind of living things once existed there. No such clues were found. All signs indicate that the Moon is, and always has been, a dead and lifeless world.

This was a great disappointment to those who believed in lunar life. But that does not mean there is no life beyond Earth, they said. They were sure that when we looked elsewhere, on Mars for example, we would find microscopic life and perhaps even larger forms.

Has life ever existed on Mars?

About a hundred years ago, belief in Martian life was popular. In 1888, Giovanni Schiaparelli, an Italian astronomer, reported that he had seen channels on Mars. The Italian word for channels is *canali.* When readers saw that word, they immediately thought of canals. If there are canals on Mars, they said, there must be intelligent creatures to build them.

Large numbers of people became convinced that there was life

During the Apollo 15 mission, Astronaut James Irwin salutes beside the American flag, with the lunar module in center and the Rover on right. NASA

Astronaut Harrison H. Schmitt is shown working with a lunar scoop during the Apollo 17 mission. NASA

on Mars. Telescopes were aimed at the target hoping to see the canals and perhaps other signs that life existed there. An American astronomer, Percival Lowell, reported that he could see many straight lines that must be canals. Some of them branched into smaller ones and probably carried water for irrigating crops. As Martian spring approached, regions along the canals darkened, just as would be expected when crops began to grow. The markings that Lowell reported were later proved not to be canals, although Lowell still insisted that they were. He even built an observatory to learn more about them.

Suspicions that life existed on Mars persisted for a hundred years afterward, right up to the 1970s when planet probes landed on Mars and sifted through the soil looking for signs of life.

On July 20, 1976, exactly seven years after men landed on the Moon, Viking 1 landed on Chryse Planitia, the Martian plain of gold. Three months later, Viking 2 landed on the Utopia Plains of Mars.

Both probes were equipped with automatic laboratories triggered by radio signals from Earth. The labs picked up Martian soil and tested it to see if gases such as carbon dioxide were given off when the soil was fed nutrients and a lamp simulating sunlight was turned on. The gas was identified. The discovery was exciting, for carbon dioxide is a gas released by living organisms. But it was not proof that life existed on Mars, because the carbon dioxide could have come from the soil itself. To be sure, organic molecules would have to be found, the kind that are in living things. Tests for these substances were negative—no organic molecules have ever been found on Mars. This may mean they do not exist there or, as some say, it may only mean they do not happen to be at those places where the Viking probes landed. However, many people believe the tests tell them enough to conclude there is no life on Mars. Others argue that we must explore more of Mars before we can say for certain whether or not the planet supports life.

Artist Don Davis's conception of the Viking spacecraft landing on the Chryse Planitia of Mars, where it explored for signs of life.
NASA

Are conditions on the other planets favorable to life?

The results of explorations of the Moon and Mars have disappointed those who believe there is life on other planets. But they do not give up easily. Even if life does not exist on these bodies, they say, it might arise at other places, such as Jupiter or Titan, one of the satellites of Saturn.

Jupiter is a likely place for life to appear eventually, for it contains methane, ammonia, hydrogen, and water—gases that are the raw materials of amino acids, which are essentials of living things. Presently, however, other conditions on the planet —such as low temperatures and lack of bodies of water—would not permit the development of life forms.

Belief in life on Titan has diminished since we have discovered that it is covered with poisonous gases such as hydrogen cyanide, and the entire satellite is a super-refrigerator. It is most unlikely that any organisms could form there.

Even though increased knowledge about places like Jupiter and Titan makes life there most improbable, living things might appear in the solar system at other locations that have not been explored.

As far as we know, living organisms need a fairly even temperature, liquid water, and life-supporting gases. Except Earth, no location in the solar system contains liquid water—large seas that remain liquid year in and year out. No location remains at a fairly even and moderate temperature throughout the year. And no location contains an atmosphere made of large amounts of nitrogen and oxygen.

In daytime, Mercury's temperature reaches 350°C. At night, it drops to 185°C below zero. It lacks an atmosphere.

Venus is always incredibly hot. Day and night, its temperature holds at 460°C; that's 860° Fahrenheit (F). The warmest that Mars gets is 28°C in summer, and this is restricted to a narrow band of the planet. Most of Mars is much colder.

The atmosphere of Venus is, for the most part, dense carbon dioxide. The Martian atmosphere, which is very thin, is also largely carbon dioxide.

The major planets—Jupiter, Saturn, Uranus, and Neptune—contain large amounts of methane and ammonia. Very likely, Pluto cannot hold an atmosphere—its gravity is not strong enough. All of the outer planets are terribly cold, with temperatures at or below 200°C below zero.

Satellites of the planets are also very cold. The exception is the Moon. During a lunar night, it is cold, 156°C below zero. But during the lunar day, its temperature soars to 132°C above zero. Such a range is far from favorable for anything alive.

When conditions anywhere in the solar system are considered carefully, even the most stubborn life-believer must agree it is most unlikely that there are living creatures on any of the planets or satellites. We appear to be alone in the solar system.

LIFE ON EARTH

What is life?

Before we go further in our discussion of the search for life, it might be a good idea to probe into the mystery of what life is and how it came about. What are we really looking for?

It should be an easy matter to decide whether or not something is alive. Just as we are certain that a cat, a tree, or a fish is alive, we are sure that a rock, an iron pipe, a drop of water, or the air around us is dead. However, it is not always easy to decide whether certain structures are alive or not. For example, viruses which are smaller than bacteria can be put aside and stored as one might store a container of sand or gravel. Should the sample be the tobacco virus, when released, the substance will enter the cells of tobacco plants and change them by causing a viral disease to develop. This will happen even after the virus has been stored for decades. Under some circumstances, the virus appears to be lifeless; whereas at other times, it is clearly alive.

In this book, we'll use certain conditions in deciding whether or not something is alive. First, it must be able to reproduce—there must be some way of making new units. The substance also must include giant molecules, especially DNA (deoxyribonucleic acid). This is the structure that carries information for the formation of new units. And there must be growth—the organism must use energy to carry out chemical reactions, such as taking in nourishment and giving off waste materials. Finally, there must be change. Over long periods of time, even millions of years, the organism must be able to evolve. Change is a condition of life.

Somewhere in the universe, it is possible there are life forms different from those we know on Earth. That is, there might be structures that appear to be alive; they might even move about. But we would not consider them to be alive unless they met all the conditions mentioned above.

We further define life by associating it with carbon. Among all the atoms, those of carbon have the greatest ability to link atoms together into complex patterns. There are more compounds of carbon than of any other substance; more than two million have been discovered or created. Each compound has its own properties. Only carbon can make the great number of substances needed to carry out the many functions of living organisms. These carbon compounds are usually water soluble. They are active in water and can be carried from place to place.

So far as we know, life depends upon the presence of carbon and liquid water. In fact, many scientists say that it doesn't make much sense to search for life anywhere that does not have large bodies of liquid water. Also, these oceans must have lasted for at least a hundred million years—the shortest time believed to be needed for nonliving substances to become living organisms.

How did life appear on Earth?

Someone has said that in order for life to appear, all that is needed are the right substances in the right amounts, the right arrangement, and the right surroundings.

That sounds simple enough. But it really poses many problems, for one must explain how all these conditions were met here on Earth. Some people avoid such problems when they propose that life did not begin here but rather in outer space somewhere, and the living organisms were transplanted here. They say the organisms might have been carried to Earth aboard meteorites that landed here billions of years ago, or even aboard comets that might have crashed into Earth. Others like to believe that civilizations far beyond Earth sent out "life capsules" millions upon millions of years ago, hoping to colonize the universe. Life would have begun where one of those capsules landed and where favorable conditions for growth existed. One of those places was Earth.

But most people believe that such transplants were unlikely. They argue that life began here on our own planet when everything was right—the substances, their amounts, their arrangement, and their surroundings.

Life has been on Earth for 3.5 billion years. We know this because that is the age of fossils of algae that were found in South Africa. Life may have taken a hundred million years to evolve from simple chemicals. Just how it came about remains a mystery, but the sequence of events may have been something like the following.

After oceans and solid continents had formed on Earth, the planet was showered with sunlight. Also, there may have been violent lightning discharges in the atmosphere, some of which reached the surface. Presently our atmosphere is made mostly of nitrogen and oxygen. But it wasn't always so. There was a time when methane and ammonia and free hydrogen were the main parts. When these gases had become mixed together with water vapor, an electrical discharge may have caused them to combine to form amino acids. These are the substances out of which proteins are made, and proteins are essential to the structure of living organisms.

Once formed, these amino acids may have been washed into the oceans, making a broth in which they survived. Various kinds of proteins may have joined together to be further bombarded by lightning discharges. At some stage, conditions and substances were just right for molecules to be formed that could reproduce themselves. The essence of life had been created.

In order for life to continue, matter and energy must flow into and out of the organism. Since the organisms formed in a broth of organic molecules, these molecules were available to them. In the absence of oxygen (there was little free oxygen available on the early Earth), the only way organisms could get the energy they required was by fermentation. A familiar modern-day example of fermentation is that of sugar by yeast in the making of bread. Carbon dioxide produced by fermentation causes the bread to rise. In the process, alcohol is given off as well as carbon dioxide. Animal cells also ferment sugar, but they release lactic acid rather than alcohol.

Early living organisms were consuming organic molecules, of which there was a limited supply. Had the organisms continued to depend upon fermentation for their energy, the molecules would have been consumed and the organisms would have died off. Ways had to be found to renew and increase the energy supply, to convert inorganic substances such as carbon, hydrogen, and water into organic molecules. Fortunately, carbon dioxide, the waste product of fermentation, was plentiful. It became key to the development of other ways to produce energy for early organisms.

Sometime during the long evolution of these organisms, photosynthesis occurred in them. Just how that happened is another mystery. Photosynthesis is the process by which an organism can produce its own organic molecules using the energy of sunlight. A basic molecule produced in the process is sugar, made from carbon dioxide and water. When nitrogen is added, an extensive selection of organic molecules can be created.

This was a tremendously important step, for now organisms could make their own organic matter. And they could ferment that matter to produce the energy they required.

But fermentation releases poisonous waste products such as alcohol and lactic acid. When living organisms were in the sea, this was no problem because the wastes were carried away. But if life were to move onto land, the poisons would accumulate and kill the organism.

As photosynthesis continued, the supply of free oxygen grew, for oxygen is a waste product of photosynthesis. When oxygen was available in the atmosphere, the organisms could obtain energy by respiration rather than fermentation. In respiration, sugar combines with oxygen to produce energy. The waste products are carbon dioxide and water, two substances easily disposed of. The carbon dioxide goes into the air, and the water flows away or is released as vapor.

Living things could now flourish. They were no longer dependent upon the infrequent creation of organic molecules. And they could produce energy in an efficient manner. In fact, they could produce more than they required. As organisms grew, they changed. Occasionally these changes yielded more complex organisms. The stage had been set for the emergence of the higher forms of life that were to become the plants and trees, insects, fish, and animals that inhabit Earth.

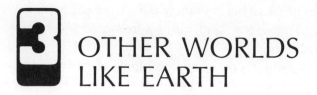

3 OTHER WORLDS LIKE EARTH

Life appeared on Earth because the right amounts of the right materials became arranged in the right way. Also, once organisms appeared, there was abundant liquid water and a fairly even temperature that was maintained for at least a hundred million years.

If these conditions should have occurred at some other location in the universe, it would be reasonable to expect that life would have started there also. Let's take a look at various parts of the universe for possible locations and the materials of life.

Are there molecules among the stars?

A strong argument for believing that life exists at other places in the universe is the presence of many kinds of molecules in the space between stars, in interstellar space. And a good many of these molecules are organic; that is, they are based upon the carbon atom just as life itself is based upon that atom. They are the same molecules that one expects would be needed to put together basic life-building molecules on Earth: the amino acids and proteins. To construct them, substances such as hydrogen cyanide, ammonia, formaldehyde, and water are needed. Molecules such as methyl alcohol are also important. All of these molecules have been detected in interstellar space.

Why the molecules exist is a mystery. Were they formed in stars? Perhaps, or they may have been formed in the same places they are now found, in tremendous clouds of organic as well as inorganic molecules. If so, they would be available on the surface of any planet in the region of those clouds. They would have to be present at the same time that other conditions are right if they are to combine into proteins and amino acids on that planet. The building of complex organic molecules may be common throughout the universe.

Where may life be found?

For one reason or another, it is unlikely that there is life anywhere else in our solar system. As explained earlier, the planets are too hot or too cold. Many contain poisonous gases or lack an atmosphere. Also, none of the planets have large amounts of water. Therefore, we must look beyond the solar system.

We must look for an object that is going around a star in the same way that Earth, Mercury, Venus, and all the other planets go around the Sun. The star must be one that is like the Sun in many ways.

When you look into a clear, dark sky, you can see about three thousand stars. With a powerful telescope, millions can be seen. But there are many more. In our family of stars, called the Milky Way galaxy, there are some 200 billion stars—so many it would take six thousand years to count them if you counted one a second.

The Sun is one of those stars. But all stars are not like the Sun; some are larger or smaller, hotter or cooler, brighter or dimmer, older or younger. Some of the stars are doubles or triples—two or three stars going around one another. Some of those stars probably have planets going around them. We have to say probably, because there is no positive proof that these alien worlds exist.

Should there be far-off worlds, we would not be able to see them. They would be much too dim. We can see distant stars because they are bright; they produce their own light. But planets do not produce light; they shine because they reflect starlight. They reflect very little, not nearly enough to penetrate the tremendous distances that separate us from them.

Beyond the Sun, the star nearest to us is Proxima Centauri. It is one of a three-star system called Alpha Centauri—the brightest star, actually a group of three stars, in the southern constellation called Centaurus (the centaur was a creature half-man and half-horse). Proxima Centauri is 4.25 light-years away. That means it takes light 4.25 years to travel to us from that star. (Light travels some 300 000 kilometers in a second; close to 9 trillion kilometers in a year.) And that's the closest star. In our galaxy, there are only eight stars within 10 light-years of us. Most of them are hundreds of thousands of light-years away.

Because of these great distances, none of our present telescopes could see a planet if it did exist, nor could any Earth-based telescope that could be developed. How then can we ever know if there are planets going around other stars?

We can tell because of the effects of gravity. Suppose there were people on a distant planet who were using sensitive instruments to observe the Sun. They would see that the Sun is moving through space, but it is not moving in an even line. At regular intervals, it moves very slightly to one side and then to the other. Because of these side-to-side movements, the observers would know that something was pulling on the Sun. It might be another star, or it might be a planet—perhaps several of them.

That's exactly what has been observed from our watching certain stars. All stars move. They might move toward us or away from us, or they might move sideways. Most of them move steadily and smoothly. However, one star about 6 light-years

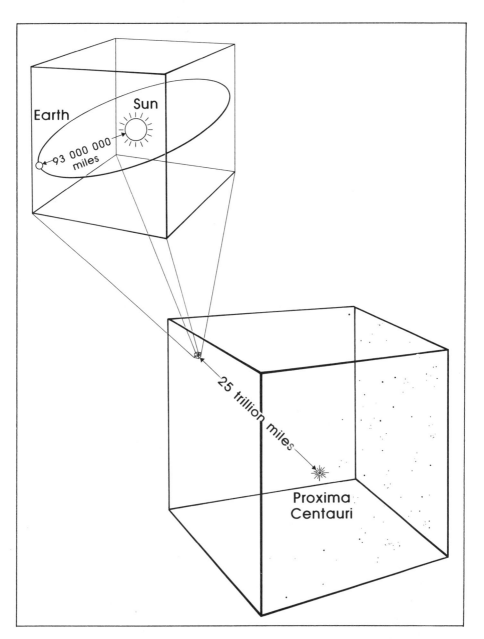

After the Sun, the star closest to Earth is Proxima Centauri. It is 4.25 light-years away.

away was noticed to be moving in a slightly different fashion. As it moved ahead, it also moved from side to side. It did not move very much, much less than one degree. (The diameter of the full Moon is one-half degree.) A cycle from one side to the other took 25 years.

This star is called Barnard's star, after Edwin E. Barnard, an astronomer who studied it back in 1916. It is in the constellation Ophiuchus, the serpent bearer, which is a rambling group of stars just above Scorpius. The amount that Barnard's star moves indicates that it has a nearby companion. Astronomers have figured out that the companion is not massive enough (it does not contain enough material) to be a star. So it has to be a planet, or several planets. It seems likely that there are two planets going around Barnard's star, one making the journey in 12 years and the other in 26 years.

If these planets do exist, it is most unlikely they would be able to support life. Barnard's star is too different from the Sun. In fact, of the forty stars closest to the Earth, only one appears to meet all the conditions needed for a star to have life-supporting planets going around it. That star is Tau Ceti, one of the dimmer stars in the constellation Cetus, the whale. It is 10.8 light-years away. However, its motion appears to be smooth, without side-to-side deflections.

Does Vega have planets?

Another reason we suspect there are planets going around some stars is the evidence supplied by IRAS, the Infrared Astronomical Satellite launched in 1983.

IRAS looked at Vega, the bright star in Lyra, a summer constellation. IRAS received infrared energy from the region, indicating there were cool objects in the vicinity of Vega—perhaps a huge cloud of solid particles. Vega is a young star, too young, it is believed, for planets to have formed about it. But this cloud of particles may eventually contract, causing the material to pack

The Infrared Astronomical Satellite (IRAS) revealed clouds of cool particles that may eventually form into planets around Vega, as well as the existence of at least forty other stars.   NASA

together into a larger object. The particles may become a planet, or many planets, in orbit around Vega. Astronomers may have seen an early stage in the formation of a planetary system. When IRAS looked at Fomalhaut, the brightest star in Piscis Austrinus, the southern fish, another similar cloud of particles was detected. Altogether, at least seven stars, and perhaps as many as forty, appear to have clouds of solid particles in their vicinity.

An especially interesting formation was found around Beta Pictoris, a dim star in Pictot, the painter's easel, a constellation in the southern sky. The star appears embedded in a dust cloud, much as Vega seems to be. Except the Pictoris cloud is disk-shaped—a disk seen from the edge. The disk extends some 60 billion miles on either side of the star, which is at least ten times greater than the extent of our solar system.

It is believed we are seeing a solar system that has developed inside the original disk. If the disk were young, most of the light of the star would be blocked. However, the star can be seen clearly. This probably means that the inner parts of the disk do not contain much dust, exactly what one would expect if much of the material had already formed into planets. In Beta Pictoris, we may be looking at a star that is surrounded by a system of planets.

What is VB8B?

VB8B is not a mysterious code but the designation of a companion of the star VB8 that appears to be a planet—a very hot one, true, but still a planet.

The star is named after Peter Van Biesbroeck, an astronomer who is credited with many discoveries. For a considerable time, VB8 was of interest because of its wobbly motion.

The formation around VB8, now called VB8B, turns out to be a ball of gases dozens of times more massive than Jupiter, with a temperature of 1100°C. That's a lot hotter than the planets familiar to us. Although it contains a great amount of material, the

formation does not have nearly enough mass to support nuclear fusion.

When stars form, a tremendous amount of material packs together—so much that temperature soars to several million degrees. At such high temperatures, nuclear fusion begins and the mass becomes a producer of energy. Smaller amounts of material become planets; the gases cool and solidify. Although Jupiter is a large planet, its mass would have to be at least one hundred times greater for it to become a star.

Likewise, VB8B is not a star.

The heat of VB8B comes from the process of formation, not from fusion. The object is still cooling, releasing heat generated when its material first packed together. VB8B is so hot that some people say it is really not a planet. They call it a brown dwarf, an object that lies somewhere between a star and a planet.

Whether it's a planet or a brown dwarf, VB8B proves that objects form around other stars. Our solar system is not that unusual. Now that scientists have reason to believe that brown dwarfs exist, they are searching for more of them. Astronomers may find many similar objects, some of which may be smaller, with masses more like that of Jupiter, which is truly a planet.

Which stars may support planets?

When you look at stars, they appear to be single points of light. And many of them are. However, with telescopes and other instruments, astronomers have found that many of the stars are really doubles or triples.

In fact, according to some astronomers, most stars have companions. These may be other stars, or they may be planets— objects of smaller mass. According to this theory, planets may be just as plentiful as stars, or even more so.

Perhaps this is true. But only a few such planets could support life. On Earth, life first appeared some 3.5 billion years ago. Therefore, it took a very long time for life to develop to its present

level. Probably it took at least 2 billion years for complex creatures of any kind to appear. If that is so, we can assume that for life to succeed, the chemical structure of a planet must not change abruptly and the temperature must remain moderate for at least 2 billion years.

What is the Nemesis star?

It seems likely that these conditions would prevail only in the vicinity of single stars, such as the Sun. We know that Earth is one of a system of planets that goes around a star. And we know that the Sun is a solitary star. Or is it?

Presently there is a theory called the Nemesis Hypothesis that says the Sun is not solitary; it is one of the stars in a two-star system. On occasion, once every 26 to 30 million years, the stars come closer together. When that happens, the companion star, called the Nemesis star, moves closer to the Oort cloud. That's a cloud of dust that surrounds our solar system. It is believed to be the source of the dust and gases that make up comets.

Nemesis pulls dust out of the Oort cloud. This dust evolves into millions of comets that are pulled toward the Sun. As they move in, many hundreds of thousands of comets rain down on Earth, generating heat and causing flash fires. The dust from these comets and fires forms a dense cloud that blots out the Sun. For decades after, Earth cools down. It gets so cold that many forms of life are destroyed. During one of these occurrences, the one that cooled the Earth 65 million years ago, the dinosaurs disappeared. According to the Nemesis Hypothesis, a visit by the Sun's companion star started the chain of events that led to the nemesis, the downfall, of the dinosaurs.

A search is on for the Nemesis star. Some astronomers believe five thousand candidate stars meet the required conditions. But is there really such a companion star? That is another mystery.

If there is a Nemesis star, then we would know that planets can form around double stars, not only around single stars as previ-

ously suspected. That would greatly increase the possibility that other planets are out there. Also, we would know that the conditions for the emergence of intelligent life could possibly exist on such planets.

Still, a planet must be located just the right distance from its star (or stars). If the planet is too close, it would be too hot for life to develop; if too far, it would be too cold. Also, the star must be one that can shine steadily for at least 2 billion years.

Not all stars do that; some last for only a few million years.

The Sun is a medium-bright, middle-aged star, just right for life to exist. Planets going around stars that are much younger and hotter would have short lives—not long enough for life to develop. Those associated with cooler and older stars would not be exposed to enough energy for life to appear.

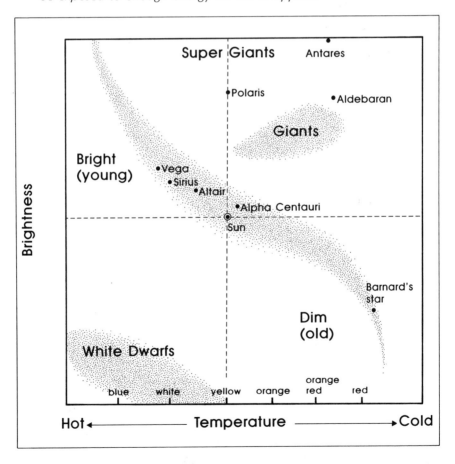

These are the very brilliant and massive blue white stars. They produce tremendous amounts of energy, so much that they burn out quickly. There would not be nearly enough time for life to evolve on any planet that might be associated with such a star. Also, the temperature would be much too high.

Many stars have extremely long lives. They may last for a hundred billion years, ten times longer than the expected lifetime of the Sun. That's plenty of time for life to develop. However, these stars with long lives are much cooler than the Sun. Planets would have to be close to them, and the range of distances for life to appear would be very narrow. Even if the planet were well-located, it is unlikely that life would begin. Apparently great amounts of energy are needed to put the "spark" to life—energy in the form of strong electrical discharges or perhaps X rays or ultraviolet radiation. Bursts of energy do not occur on these cool, long-lasting stars. So, if planets should move around them, chances are these planets would be cold, desolate, and lifeless worlds.

It would seem that only Sun-like stars have the proper lifetimes and temperature ranges for life to appear and develop. About 10 percent of the stars in our galaxy are like the Sun, or close to it. That would mean there are at least 20 billion locations in the Milky Way galaxy where these conditions might exist. Just where they are remains a mystery.

OTHER SYSTEMS OF STARS AND PLANETS

Even if all conditions were favorable, many people think it most unlikely that intelligent creatures like those on Earth have appeared anywhere else in the universe. Even if life began elsewhere, it is most improbable, they say, that it would have developed in exactly the same way that life developed here. The possibility that humans appeared anywhere else, they say, is about as great as the chance that monkeys aimlessly tapping at typewriters would eventually compose *Romeo and Juliet* or any of the other plays of William Shakespeare.

They may be right; Earth may be the only place where there are intelligent creatures. But they may be wrong. In our galaxy there may be millions of planets that support advanced civilizations. Beyond our galaxy, there are billions of other galaxies. In each, there may be additional millions of planets supporting intelligent life. This is not a new idea. In the 4th century B.C., a philosopher named Metrodorus said, "To consider Earth as the only populated world in infinite space is as absurd as to assert that in an entire field sown with millet only one grain will grow." If there are such civilizations, how are we to know they exist?

What are Earth-based clues to life?

Back in the days when people believed there were Martians watching us, and before the days of radio telescopes, many people wondered how we could let Martians know that intelligent creatures lived on Earth. Many suggestions were made using mathematics, a "language" that would be the same everywhere. For example, a triangle is a shape that any intelligent person would know about. If the Martians saw a precise triangle on our planet, they might guess that intelligent creatures made it. One idea was to plant wide rows of trees in a triangle with each side several miles long. Wheat would be planted inside the triangle to make a large, light area that would contrast with the dark trees.

Another plan using a triangle proposed that three squares of wheat be planted, using each side of a right triangle as a side for one of the squares. This would illustrate the rule known by mathematicians everywhere that the square of the hypotenuse equals the sum of the squares of the other two sides. The relationship is shown in the right triangle in the drawing.

A third plan was to dig channels in the form of a triangle across the Sahara desert. At night, kerosene in the channels would be set afire. The light would stand out sharply against the dark sky and so would be visible from Mars.

None of these plans were ever tried out. We suspect, however, that a good many observers surmised that if we had such ideas, the Martians would also have thought about them. No doubt there were people who spent long hours hoping to see tell-tale triangles on the red planet.

How can radio astronomy help?

Presently the search for life goes far beyond Mars, even beyond the solar system. Until the 1950s, very little was done to actively search for life beyond Earth. It was then that radio astronomy began to be developed. Antennas were able to pick up radio

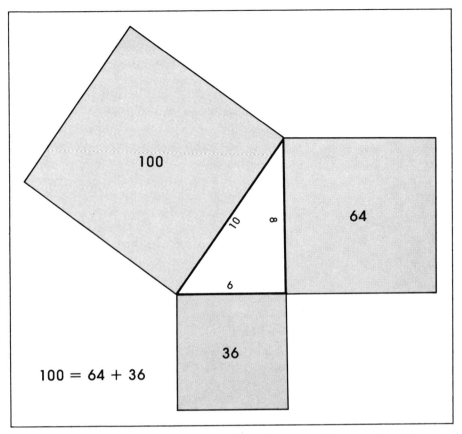

Intelligent beings throughout the universe would recognize this triangle pattern which demonstrates that the square of the hypotenuse equals the sum of the squares of the other two sides.

waves from outer space, much as optical telescopes picked up light waves. When an object such as a star is energetic, it gives off energy in the form of X rays, ultraviolet rays, and light and radio waves. Radio waves contain the least amount of energy. Less energetic stars, the radio stars, give off mainly radio waves. Individual atoms also give off radio waves. The waves penetrate through space much more so than do light waves. All these waves are natural phenomena; people are not involved in their creation. In addition, there are man-made waves, those that carry our radio and TV programs.

Since the 1920s, when radio broadcasting became popular, we have been making radio waves. And they have been going out into space. By now the waves have traveled some 60 or 70 light-years. You recall that a light-year is the distance that light travels in a year. A "radio year" is the same distance, for the speed of radio waves is the same as that of light waves. Perhaps a radio telescope on some planet 60 or 70 light-years from us has already intercepted one of our early programs.

Such a possibility is very exciting to radio astronomers. Since we are sending out radio waves, they said, perhaps other planets are doing the same thing. What we should do is turn our antennas toward the most likely locations. And that's what we did. For 150 hours in 1960, a radio telescope was turned to receive radio waves from the vicinity of two stars. One of these was Tau Ceti, the Sun-like star in Cetus, the whale. The other star was Epsilon Eridani, a star much like the Sun and located in the constellation Eridanus, the river, so named because it wanders around the sky like a river.

The hope was that radio waves that were produced intentionally by alien people would be picked up by our radio telescopes.

One of the problems in searching for such radio waves is tuning the receiver. A radio telescope has to be tuned to receive certain waves just as a radio has to be tuned to receive waves sent out by a certain station. Astronomers knew that there were waves in space that have a wavelength of 21 centimeters, or a frequency of 1420 megacycles. (Our radio receivers have a range of about 500 to 1600 kilocycles; the frequency of television waves is much greater—88 to 108 megacycles.)

Hydrogen atoms were identified as the transmitters of these 21-centimeter waves. Since hydrogen is the most common material in the universe, the 21-centimeter wave became the universal wavelength. It seemed logical that if anyone was trying to send out information, they would put it on this wave.

Astronomers tuned their telescopes to the 21-centimeter wave, hoping they would detect slight man-made variations in the signal. There were none.

Since this first exploration in 1960, American astronomers as well as those in other countries have continued the work. They have tuned their receivers to the universal wavelength, and also to others. So far, no radio waves except those produced naturally have been received.

Astronomers have aimed their telescopes at various stars in addition to Tau Ceti and Epsilon Eridani. That's one of the problems: which stars should they aim at? There are millions of stars out there. What wavelengths should be used, and which stars should be the targets? Alien people might use the hydrogen wave, but they might use a different one. Also, alien people might not transmit all the time. They might send out signals for only a few hours and then shut down for a long interval. To pick up radio signals sent out by other worlds, our telescopes must be pointed at just the right star at the right moment, and they must be tuned to the right waves.

How powerful are advanced radio telescopes?

Bigger and better telescopes would help. The larger a telescope is, the more sensitive it becomes. That is, large antennas can pick up weak signals that small telescopes cannot. Also, large telescopes focus more tightly. For example, suppose a telescope were aimed at the Moon. A small one might be able to pick up signals from a broad region on the surface. A large telescope could pick up signals from a region as small as a minor crater.

Large single antennas have been built. The largest is in a natural bowl at Arecibo in Puerto Rico. It is 305 meters across. The telescope is fixed, meaning that it cannot be steered. However, as Earth turns, the telescope can survey a large portion of the sky as it passes by.

A large dish antenna, some 200 meters across, is located at

The Arecibo telescope is 305 meters across. It was built into a natural bowl in the hills of Puerto Rico.   *NASA*

Green Bank, West Virginia. This telescope can be turned to cover the sky to the north and south. And it can be tuned sharply, to separate out one particular wavelength.

Yet even the best and biggest radio telescopes cannot focus as sharply as can optical telescopes. In order to do so, radio telescopes would have to be hundreds, even thousands of kilometers across. It is quite impossible to construct such a large instrument. However, telescopes mounted several miles apart can act as though they were a single instrument. One such arrangement is the Very Large Array (VLA) telescope located in New Mexico. It is made of twenty-seven telescopes, each of which is 25 meters in diameter. They are mounted on three tracks that form a Y. Computers keep the telescopes lined up on a target, enabling all twenty-seven to act as though they were one telescope some 40 kilometers across.

These telescopes, as well as others in the United States, Canada, Russia, England, and Australia, are scanning the stars. There may be millions of transmissions from many civilizations out there. But unless a telescope is pointed at a source and unless it is tuned to the correct wavelength, no signal would be detected. We need powerful telescopes, and many of them, to cover even a small part of the number of stars that could conceivably support intelligent, signal-sending civilizations.

What instruments are planned for the future?

Some people have suggested that we should build a super radio telescope. It would be an arrangement of a thousand or more dish antennas. All would operate as a single large telescope that would be extremely sensitive and so be able to pick up very weak signals. The telescope would be named Cyclops, after the legendary one-eyed giant.

Such an array of telescopes would be very expensive. And, even though it would be sensitive, it would still have to overcome interference caused by waves generated on Earth. It might be

Scientists are using this radio telescope at the Harvard-Smithsonian Observatory in their search for other civilizations. Any signals received by the telescope are recorded, and it is hoped that one day the telescope will receive a signal generated by extraterrestrials. *HARVARD-SMITHSONIAN CENTER FOR ASTRO-PHYSICS*

The Cyclops instrument would be made of a thousand or more telescopes all tuned to the same transmission. NASA

more effective, many people believe, to spend the money on a telescope located in outer space. This might turn out to be even more expensive, but such a telescope would be shielded from Earth-based waves and it could be very large. In space, objects are weightless and so an antenna can be built without heavy supporting braces. Sections of the telescope could be carried into space aboard shuttles. Once there, astronauts could assemble the sections and put the telescope into operation. Since the dish would be facing away from Earth, the receiver would be shielded from Earth-produced waves. There would be no interference, making it possible for such a telescope to be more sensitive than the best Earth-based instruments.

Signals picked up by the telescope would be amplified and then transmitted to receivers located on Earth. We might also consider a system of two space-based radio telescopes separated by several thousand kilometers. Computer hookups would enable the two instruments to be directed at a single target. The process of focusing two or more instruments on a target is called interferometry. The very long baseline, the distance between the instruments, would make them extremely powerful.

Many astronomers believe this is the way we should move. According to them, these telescopes would be more capable of detecting alien civilizations than any other kind of instrument. However, optical telescopes located in space are also effective. Some are already in operation.

What is the Hubble Space Telescope?

Several small optical telescopes have been put into orbit. They have given us clear pictures of the outer planets and considerable information about the Sun. But bigger and better telescopes are needed. During the rest of this century, the 12-ton Hubble optical

The large space telescope will be carried into space aboard a shuttle. NASA

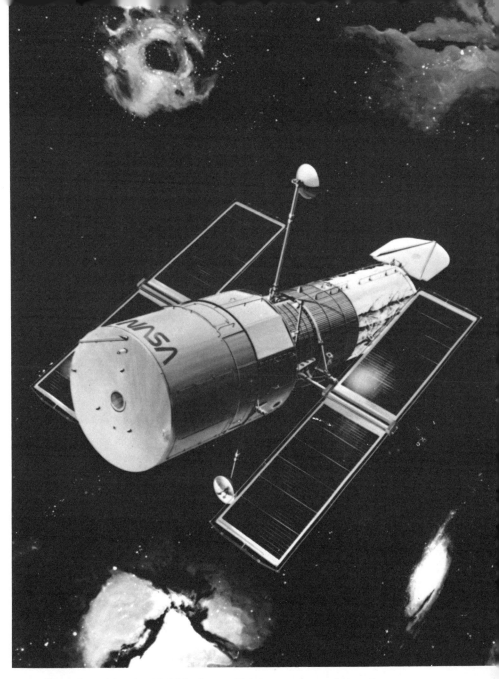

Once in orbit, the Hubble Space Telescope, free of the distortions of Earth's atmosphere, will provide astronomers with a clear view of the universe. NASA telescope, with a mirror 2.4 meters (94.5 inches) across, will be operating soon after its launch by a space shuttle.

The orbit will be 500 kilometers above Earth's surface. Because of weightlessness and the absence of air, the telescope will respond readily to radio controls from Earth. Because the instrument is held steady, it will be possible to take clear long-exposure photographs. Data gathered by the telescope will be transmitted to Earth stations. Day to day operation of the telescope will be by space command. And astronauts will be able to visit the instrument or bring it into the cargo bay of a shuttle to make repairs and adjustments should they be needed. Regular maintenance should keep the Hubble Space Telescope operating well into the twenty-first century.

The telescope will be able to detect objects much dimmer than those that can be seen by the 5-meter (200-inch) Hale telescope on Mount Palomar. Even though the images may be only one-hundredth as bright, the Hubble telescope will pick them up. As it continues to gather information in the decades ahead, the telescope will expand our reach into space many times farther.

Eventually, it may reveal the presence of planets going around distant stars. That alone would make the venture worthwhile. In addition, it will see distant galaxies more clearly; it will see conditions as they existed billions of years ago—perhaps shortly after the start of the universe. It may give us valuable information regarding other mysteries astronomers wonder about—quasars, pulsars, and black holes. So even if the space telescope does not collect evidence of the existence of alien worlds, it will bring us a lot closer to understanding the structure and history of the universe.

What is optical interferometry?

Interferometry is a system using two or more telescopes to zero in on a target. We already mentioned radio interferometry. The effect is as though there were a single large telescope, one as large as the distance between the two instruments.

Sometime in the 1990s, there may be two or more large optical telescopes in Earth orbit, providing optical interferometry from space. They will be interconnected by means of computers and lasers, and so will provide an incredible ability to see separate parts of star groups and to detect the slightest variations in the motions of individual stars. The space telescope also performs these functions, but this system for the 1990s or early twenty-first century would be several times more sensitive.

Astronomers believe that such an arrangement of space-based instruments would be able to study every star in the Sun's neighborhood, and so provide an accurate survey of the possible existence of solar systems throughout that region.

What are optical super-telescopes?

Additionally, there is considerable excitement about the construction in the 1990s of two land-based optical super-telescopes: one to be located in Hawaii and the other, probably, in Arizona. They should both be operating before the end of the century.

Presently the largest optical telescopes are the 5-meter Hale telescope on Mount Palomar in California and the 6-meter telescope in the Caucasus mountains of the Soviet Union. These instruments can look out to a distance of roughly 8 billion light-years. The new telescopes are designed to have a range of 12 billion light-years. They should be able to see the universe as it was soon after the Big Bang from which it is believed the universe was formed.

The telescope to be erected in Hawaii will be a 10-meter instrument. It will be made of several smaller mirrors that will be computer integrated to produce the light-gathering ability of a single 10-meter mirror. Each segment of the telescope, called the Keck telescope after the foundation that paid for it, will be regu-

This model is a replica of the NNTT (National New Technology Telescope), which will enable scientists to see further into space than ever before. NATIONAL OPTICAL ASTRONOMY OBSERVATORIES

lated so the tilt will be modified three hundred times a second.

The Arizona telescope, called the NNTT (National New Technology Telescope), will be 15 meters. It will be built and controlled by the National Optical Astronomy Observatories in Tucson, Arizona. It will be made of four 7.5-meter mirrors. It had been believed that 5 meters was the largest mirror that could be made. However, a technique was developed at the Observatories that permits perfect mirrors of 7.5 meters to be fabricated.

No one knows what these super-telescopes will discover. They will certainly see farther back in time than we have been able to up to this moment. So they may reveal the way the universe used to be. We will then be able to extend our knowledge about the evolution of the universe. Through such knowledge, we may obtain further insights about how life might have appeared and how it might have evolved, not only on Earth but at locations other than our own.

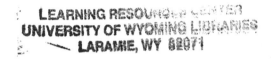

SPACE COLONIES TO STARSHIPS

Advanced optical and radio telescopes may give us positive evidence that there are planets going around distant stars. Radio telescopes may pick up tell-tale signals that originated on such planets. Should that happen, and we were confident that intelligent creatures were out there, our efforts would be toward communicating with them. Ultimately we would want to go to that planet—land on a foreign world, meet the inhabitants, and learn about their civilization and its history. The first steps have already been taken.

Have signals been sent into space?

In 1974, as part of the dedication ceremonies of the Arecibo radio telescope, the telescope sent a coded message out toward a large cluster of stars in the constellation Hercules. The cluster is 25 000 light-years away—it will take that long for the message to reach its destination. Should there be creatures at that location who wish to send a reply, the response would reach us 50 000 years from 1974. The location was chosen because there are

The Arecibo Message of 1974

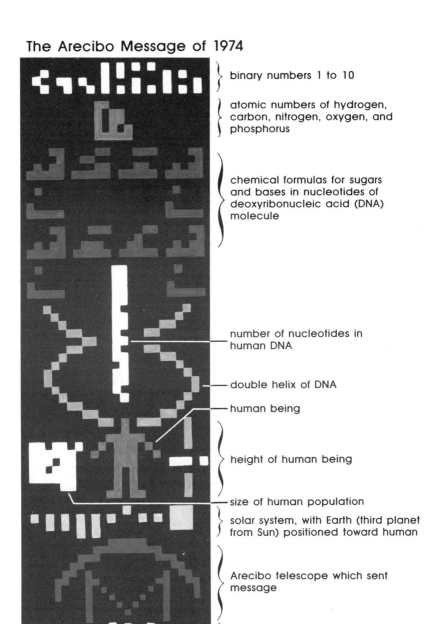

binary numbers 1 to 10

atomic numbers of hydrogen, carbon, nitrogen, oxygen, and phosphorus

chemical formulas for sugars and bases in nucleotides of deoxyribonucleic acid (DNA) molecule

number of nucleotides in human DNA

double helix of DNA

human being

height of human being

size of human population

solar system, with Earth (third planet from Sun) positioned toward human

Arecibo telescope which sent message

diameter of telescope

Radiogram sent to Hercules   NATIONAL ASTRONOMY AND ION-OSPHERE CENTER

thousands of stars in the group, and so there would be many more chances the message would be detected than if it had been directed toward a single star.

The message was sent in a series of pulses which, when decoded, would produce the design shown in the illustration. As you can see, it contains a great deal of information.

As mentioned earlier, our TV programs of the past several decades are also moving out into space. But they contain no messages designed to give information about us to alien people.

What are the Pioneer plaques?

The Arecibo message sent toward Hercules is a radio signal. In addition, we have sent into space objects that will leave the solar system and move into interstellar space. Two of these are the Pioneers.

In 1972 and 1973, two planet probes, Pioneer 10 and 11, were launched from Earth. A message-bearing plaque is attached to each probe. The first probe went near Jupiter, and the second made a close approach to Saturn. Both of the Pioneers coasted to the planets and then were speeded up by gravity of the planets. The speed of the probes became great enough for them to escape from the Sun's gravitational attraction. Both are now traveling in orbits that will carry them into space between the stars. At some time in the future, perhaps thousands or more years from now, the Pioneers may approach other stars. Going around some of those stars, there may be planets inhabited by intelligent creatures. If so, the Pioneers may be intercepted by them.

It is assumed that if there are alien people, they would be at least as intelligent as we are, and so be able to figure out the message that is fastened to the Pioneers. One of the gold-coated aluminum plaques carried by them is shown in the drawing. Hopefully, aliens would know from the information at the bottom of the plaque that Pioneer came from a planet—the third from the Sun. And from the center left, they would know that the Sun

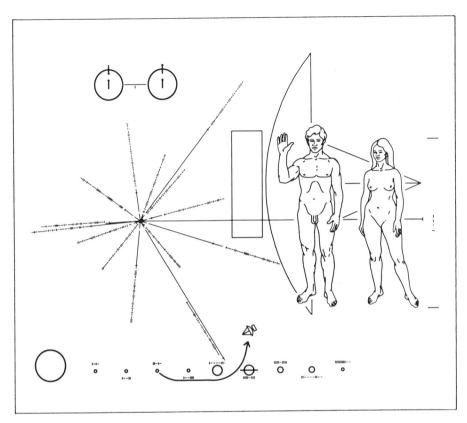

A Pioneer plaque NASA

is located at a point in space from which pulsars with certain frequencies are located at particular distances.

What messages are aboard Voyager?

Two Voyager probes investigated Jupiter and its satellites and also Saturn and its satellites. Voyager 2 went on to study Uranus in 1986. As with the Pioneers, the Voyager missions were to make close approaches to the planets, which they did. Gravity of the planets speeded the probes, acting as slingshots to accelerate them to escape velocity—the speed needed to escape from the

Sun's gravitation. The Voyagers are now on their way to the outer planets. They will then continue outward, leaving the solar system and embarking on a journey that may continue for thousands of years.

Fastened to the outside of each Voyager is a record containing sounds of Earth, including voices of people, rock and classical music, and greetings from the president of the United States. There are coded signals which, when fed into a TV-like converter, produce pictures of Earth—people, animals, the DNA molecule, plants, deserts, mountains, fish, shells, and insects. There is also information that would help aliens figure out where the Voyagers came from.

Who knows? One day people way out among the stars may receive the Arecibo message, or they may intercept a Pioneer or Voyager probe. If they do, chances are they would try to communicate with us. They may already have done so if they have received our old radio and TV programs.

How will space stations aid the search for life?

Space stations will help in many ways, and we have taken the first steps toward them. The beginning came in 1961 when Yuri I. Gagarin, the Russian cosmonaut, went into orbit around Earth. After that, both the United States and Russia put many more men and women into space, and the United States landed twelve men on the Moon in the Apollo program.

Crews have spent months aboard space stations such as our Skylab and the Soviet's Salyut and Mir installations. They have proved that humans can survive for long periods, even though they are weightless. When Skylab was launched, serious troubles developed with the solar collector and the sunshade. The troubles were corrected by astronauts working outside the vehicle. It was proved that men could work in outer space. It was shown on other occasions as well—dramatically when astronauts recovered Solar Max, repaired the satellite, and then put it back into orbit.

Experience has shown that with proper preparation, life can be sustained in outer space. And, more than that, productive work can be completed.

The costs of these explorations have been very high. Before the shuttles, rocket engines used to launch men and vehicles were not reusable. A vehicle was used once, then it was discarded—never returned to Earth. A comparable situation would be to fly a plane from New York to London once and then throw it away.

The better way is to design a launch vehicle that can be returned, repaired if necessary, and then used for another mission. That's what space shuttles do. They are built so that a single ship can make scores of journeys carrying equipment into space and then return to Earth. Cost is still very high. Hopefully, as shuttles continue to be developed, costs will come down.

By 1986, shuttles had made twenty-four successful flights. Then, on January 28, 1986, the Challenger shuttle blew up during launch and, tragically, the entire crew of seven men and women were lost. Intense investigations followed, to find the cause of the accident. It was found to be in connectors of sections of the solid rocket boosters which cannot function properly in cold weather. This is a condition about which engineers had warned officials several times. However, the officials did not heed the warnings. Even though the temperature at the Florida launch site was around freezing on that day, the countdown proceeded. The O-rings connecting sections of the rocket boosters did not seal completely. Hot gases escaped and ignited fuel in the main tank, causing the explosion.

The shuttle program was then put on hold: No launches would take place until everything was corrected and until NASA was reorganized. Once operating again, shuttles will proceed with the national program of space exploration.

Shuttles are remarkable; they can carry 30 tons in the cargo bay, which is 18 meters long and 5 meters across, large enough to carry prefabricated sections of space stations. Once these sections are in orbit, astronauts will fasten them together. In the 1990s, we can expect that stations housing up to eight scientists and engineers will be built. Among the people aboard will be astronomers who will continue to explore the outer universe in search of signs of life.

Presently, plans are developing to have a space station operating sometime in 1994. It will be built out of modules, or sections, carried by shuttles and then assembled in orbit. Astronauts aboard the station will repair satellites, launch vehicles to higher orbits, tend manufacturing operations, and assemble additional modules for such things as power stations, space telescopes, and space factories.

During the 1990s, a space station, like this one in many ways, will be constructed out of modules carried into orbit by shuttles.
ROCKWELL INTERNATIONAL

Space shuttles will be used to make large structures in space, such as this proposed satellite power system, leading to stations that can house scores of people. NASA

These stations will be stages toward space colonies that may be developed as we move into the early years of the next century. Colonies will be able to house hundreds of people, and perhaps several thousand.

These colonies, located some 200 000 kilometers from Earth, will become self-supporting. People will produce their own food; air and water will be recycled; and, eventually, colony civilizations will evolve. In the beginning, essential materials will be obtained from Earth. After some time, however, a colony will fill many of its basic needs by mining the Moon. And, as some have suggested, asteroids may also be mined for the essential materials contained in them.

Once we have operating space stations and colonies, further

In the future, thousands of people will be living in space colonies that may look like these. They will be in an especially good location to search for other civilizations in the universe. NASA **55**

exploration will be much easier to accomplish. This is largely because very little effort is needed to propel objects into space from such locations. No gigantic engines are required because escape velocity, the speed needed for objects to get away from the launching base, is very low. Although engines need be only low-powered, they must burn for a long time; acceleration is lower, but it is spread over a longer period of time.

One hoped-for mission is a manned landing on Mars. The planet continues to challenge scientists to explain its history and the changes that have occurred there. Remote labs have given us a lot of information. Also, we have information from what may be Mars rocks. These are specimens that were found in Antarctica. Some people believe they were ejected from Mars some 180 million years ago. Perhaps so. But such objects only tease those scientists who would like to visit the planet firsthand.

Will we ever have starships?

People living in space colonies will no doubt be curious about space beyond. They will wonder about life out among the stars, just as we do today. It's reasonable to expect that they will eventually devise ways to leave the solar system and set out upon journeys that will go on and on. Generations of people will come and go while the ship continues its mission among the stars, seeking civilizations that may flourish in the depths of the universe.

Mankind is an infant form of life. Humans have been on our planet only a few million years. That's not very long. Compared to the age of the dinosaurs, it is just a moment; dinosaurs dominated the planet for a hundred million years.

During our stay, we have learned how to make brief journeys into space. As mankind matures, no doubt ways will be found to live at locations other than Earth, at first in colonies close to Earth, but eventually farther away. Just as we have found ways to explore various parts of Earth, future generations will find ways to journey into the far reaches of the universe. At some date in the future, humans will very likely reach out to creatures on some distant planet, both then realizing they are not alone.

One day, ships fabricated in space will make endless journeys into the universe, seeking civilizations that may flourish among the stars. NASA

FURTHER READING

Branley, Franklyn M. *Columbia and Beyond: The Story of the Space Shuttle.* New York: Putnam, 1979.

————. *Mysteries of Outer Space.* New York: Lodestar Books, 1985.

————. *Mysteries of the Universe.* New York: Lodestar Books, 1984.

————. *Space Colony: Frontier of the 21st Century.* New York: Lodestar Books, 1982.

Moche, Dinah L. *Life in Space.* New York: A & W Publishers, 1979.

Moore, Patrick. *Travellers in Space and Time.* New York: Doubleday, 1984.

Morrison, Philip, et al. *The Search for Extraterrestrial Intelligence.* New York: Dover, 1979.

INDEX

Page numbers in *italics* refer to captions.

ABOUT THE AUTHOR

FRANKLYN M. BRANLEY is the popular author of more than 125 books for young people about astronomy and other sciences. His books include *Halley: Comet 1986, Space Colony, Jupiter,* and three other books in the Mysteries of the Universe Series.

Dr. Branley is Astronomer Emeritus and former chairman of The American Museum–Hayden Planetarium. He and his wife live in Sag Harbor, New York.

ABOUT THE ILLUSTRATOR

SALLY J. BENSUSEN is a science illustrator. Her work appears in the other books in the Mysteries of the Universe Series and *Halley: Comet 1986.* She has done illustrations for the Smithsonian as well as for many science magazines. She lives in Washington, D.C.